The ART of the

BAR
CART

The ART *of the* BAR CART

STYLING & RECIPES

VANESSA DINA

Text by **Ashley Rose Conway**
Photographs by **Antonis Achilleos**

CHRONICLE BOOKS
SAN FRANCISCO

Library of Congress Cataloging-in-Publication Data

Names: Dina, Vanessa, author. | Conway, Ashley Rose, writer of supplementary
    textual content.
Title: The art of the bar cart / Vanessa Dina ; text by Ashley Rose Conway ;
    photographs by Antonis Achilleos.
Description: San Francisco : Chronicle Books, [2017]
Identifiers: LCCN 2016051294 | ISBN 9781452158952 (hc : alk. paper)
Subjects: LCSH: Bars (Furniture) | Handcarts. | Cocktails.
Classification: LCC TT197.5.B3 D57 2017 | DDC 684.1—dc23 LC record
    available at https://lccn.loc.gov/2016051294

Manufactured in China

Design by **VANESSA DINA**
Prop styling by **ED GALLAGHER**
Text by **ASHLEY ROSE CONWAY**

10 9 8 7 6 5 4 3 2 1

Chronicle books and gifts are available at special
quantity discounts to corporations, professional associ-
ations, literacy programs, and other organizations. For
details and discount information, please contact our
corporate/premiums department at corporatesales@
chroniclebooks.com or at 1-800-759-0190.

Chronicle Books LLC
680 Second Street
San Francisco, California 94107
WWW.CHRONICLEBOOKS.COM

CONTENTS

INTRODUCTION

Bar carts are key decor pieces, whether you entertain often or just like a quiet drink at the end of a long day. There are as many ways to incorporate them into your home as there are spaces to put them. And it's not just about the cocktails; a bar cart is a statement piece as well as a functional one. A well-styled bar cart can pull together a room while providing a place to display your favorite spirits, bar tools, and glassware for making drinks. Whether roving or stationary, petite or sizable, there is a cart for everyone. That's where this book comes in.

Each cart focuses on one spirit or theme, or on creating a bar set-up in a small or unusual space. You can pick one that fits your lifestyle or mix and match to make a unique cart that is just for you. There are carts for beer and wine lovers, as well as single-liquor carts that will show you how to make the most of your favorite bottle. If you're looking to throw a party, there are carts for that. And even if you think there isn't space in your home for one more stick of furniture, the Tray Cart (page 105) and After-Eight Cart (page 123) make it easy to incorporate a home bar into the space you already have. With each cart you'll find a cocktail recipe and variations that match the theme and require only a few liquors and liqueurs, making it easier and more wallet friendly to make drinks at home. And a lot of those bottles are used repeatedly throughout the book, so you can try cocktails from other carts without having to invest in a whole new set of ingredients. For easy serving, remember that every recipe yields one drink unless otherwise noted.

When it comes to bar carts, the only rule is to make sure it works for your space. The ideas in this book are simply suggestions—jumping off points for styling and enjoying your home bar cart. Draw inspiration from the different styles and spirits you find, discover new favorite cocktail recipes, and then make them your own!

BAR BASICS

Below are some guidelines and fundamentals for making a proper cocktail. Whole books have been written on how to mix up the best drink. If you are interested in perfecting your cocktail skills, keep exploring. It's easy to customize your choices once you have an idea of which cocktails you prefer to mix up on a regular basis.

A quick note on quality: great cocktails start with great ingredients. Always use the highest quality spirits, mixers, and produce you can afford. I mix with organic fruits and vegetables whenever possible, focusing on what is in season for the best flavors. While I may want strawberries in January, I wait until early summer, when local strawberries are ripe. When you can, use fresh juices in drinks. It involves a little more work than opening a bottle, but your tipple will be far tastier. This is particularly important for citrus juice, which loses its brightness within a day of being juiced.

TOOLS

Tools do not make the man or woman, or bartender, but they sure do help in crafting a delicious drink. These are the must-have tools for the home bartender to keep on the bar cart:

- bar spoon
- bottle opener
- citrus peeler
- cocktail shaker
- ice molds in varying sizes
- jigger for measuring liquids
- mixing glass
- strainers: Hawthorne for shaken cocktails,
  julep for stirred drinks, and fine-mesh or tea for double straining

If you are looking to expand your tool selection, here are a few more tools I like to keep on hand:

- blender

- canvas Lewis bag and wooden mallet for crushing ice

- channel knife and zester combined

- muddler

- picks for garnishes

- reusable metal straws

- swizzle sticks

ICE

Ice is a key player in cocktails. They would not be as tasty or inviting without the chill that ice provides, whether it's large, small, hand cut, crystal clear, cubed, or crushed. In addition, shaking or stirring with ice adds a bit of water to a drink, which improves the flavor of many cocktails.

If you enjoy serving cocktails with crushed ice, consider investing in a Lewis bag and mallet, and crush it by hand. A Lewis bag is made of triple-stitched canvas, so you're unlikely to pop a seam with enthusiastic smashing, and the bag will absorb any water from ice melt. Crushing ice by hand ensures that you get the size you're looking for.

Speaking of size, there are many types of ice molds on the market, and they come in various dimensions. Silicone ice trays make it easier to remove the ice without cracking it, like plastic versions do. If you like drinks on the rocks, jumbo, slow-melting spheres and cubes will keep your spirit from becoming watery; try 2-in [5-cm] ones. But if you prefer to use a collins glass, or other tall, thin glassware, smaller ice cubes may be a better option. A fan of refreshing tropical drinks? Small pebble ice trays are perfect; unlike crushed ice, they won't dilute the drink too much.

STIR OR SHAKE

There is a time and place for everything, including when to stir and when to shake your cocktail. Shaking is the most commonly used method for libations containing more than liquor. It dilutes while adding air and thus texture to the drink. On the other hand, stirring adds minimal water and air, keeping the texture of the drink smooth. Spirit-heavy drinks, like a martini, are better stirred, not shaken, no matter what you may have heard.

THE ART OF STIRRING

A thick mixing glass, bar spoon, and Julep strainer are the vital tools to properly stir your drink. Pre-chill your mixing glass in the fridge or freezer if you can. Next, add ice to fill the mixing glass ⅔ of the way and add your liquid ingredients. Now, time to stir. Holding the bar spoon in-between your thumb and your index and middle fingers, place the spoon between the ice and the side of the glass without touching the bottom. The key is to stir without adding too much air and bubbles; keep the bar spoon spinning along the edge of the glass without interrupting the ice. For the best dilution and chill, aim for 30 seconds of constant stirring. Then place a Julep strainer over the mouth of the mixing glass and strain into a glass.

THE ART OF SHAKING

Shaking requires a little more finesse than stirring. The first thing to think about is the shaker. Cobbler shakers—which come with a tin, strainer, and fitted top—are popular for their classic look and are easy to find. Boston shakers—which consist of a mixing glass and tin or two tins that fit together—are more versatile and can be easier to use, although they don't have the same classic look. If you choose a Boston shaker, you will also need a separate strainer to strain out ice and solid ingredients. Both shakers are perfectly fine tools to shake up a cocktail, so pick whichever one suits your home bar.

When it comes to shaking, there are two techniques: wet shaking, which includes ice, and dry shaking, which does not. For a wet shake, combine the ingredients in the shaker and add enough ice to fill it ¾ of the way. For the best chilling and dilution for most drinks, shake for 15 seconds, unless the recipe calls for more, such as the Creamsicle Fizz on page 94.

A dry shake is used when egg whites are involved. The egg whites add a lovely foam and texture to a cocktail without adding flavor. To get them nice and foamy, shake without ice for about 1 minute, which will whip the proteins in the egg whites. Then add ice and do a wet shake to chill and dilute the drink, and strain it into a glass. (For more about strainers, see below.)

STRAINERS

There are a few different options, depending on what style drink you are mixing up. A Hawthorne strainer, which has a spring on its underside, fits on the mouth of a shaker and will keep chunks of ice, fruit, and herbs from slipping into the glass. It's also the strainer of choice after you've shaken egg whites, because it won't deflate all the lovely bubbles. Julep strainers perform a similar function for cocktails that are stirred. They fit inside the mouth of a mixing glass. Tea strainers and larger fine-mesh strainers are held over a glass to keep out pulp and other solids. You can use any of these to strain a drink, so use whatever works for your cocktail. To double strain, use a Hawthorne strainer and a fine-mesh strainer together to strain any solids out of your drink.

SYRUPS

Sugar is crucial for cocktail making; most drinks require some sweetness to balance other flavors. The best way to sweeten a drink is with a syrup, since it is incorporated more easily than sugar or honey. In this book you'll find three main types: A simple syrup, a mixture of equal parts sugar and water. An infused syrup, a simple syrup combined with herbs, spices, or produce to impart some additional flavor to the finished syrup. And honey syrup, made with honey and water. Some recipes in this book call for either simple syrup or honey syrup. Recipes that call for simple syrup can use an infused syrup instead.

SIMPLE SYRUP

Makes 12 oz [355 ml]

8 oz [240 ml] water

1 cup [200 g] sugar (white, brown, or turbinado)

1. Combine the water and sugar in a small saucepan. Bring to a boil over high heat and immediately remove from the heat.

2. Let cool and store in a sealed container in the fridge for up to 1 month.

INFUSED SYRUP

Makes 1½ to 2 cups [360 to 480 ml]

8 oz [240 ml] water

1 cup [200 g] sugar (white, brown, or turbinado)

About 1 lb [300 to 400 g] chopped fruits or vegetables, about 1 cup [35 g] fresh herbs, about 3 Tbsp dried herbs, or 2 tsp spices, in any combination

1. Combine the water and sugar in a medium saucepan and warm over high heat. When the sugar is dissolved, add your choice of produce, herbs, and spices. You can add just one or combine all of them to create a complex flavor. Bring to a boil and remove from the heat.

2. Let cool and then strain through a fine-mesh strainer. Store in a sealed container in the fridge for up to 1 month.

HONEY SYRUP

Makes 8 oz [240ml]

1 cup [340 g] honey

4 oz [120 ml] water

1. Combine the honey and water in a small saucepan and warm over medium heat until well combined.

2. Let cool and store in a sealed container in the fridge for 1 to 2 months.

GARNISHES

We drink with our eyes as well as our taste buds. That's where garnishes come in. Choose something as simple as an orange twist or as elaborate as a tiki garnish with every fruit under the sun piled on; just don't forget to garnish your drink! Aside from visual appeal, garnishes also provide aromatics, and since a large part of what we taste is affected by what we smell, garnishes add another level of flavor without adding volume to a drink. Most of the recipes in this book include garnish suggestions, which will enhance the flavors in the drink and also get you thinking about different ways to incorporate garnishes into your cocktails.

GLASSWARE

If the ingredients are the cocktail stars, glassware is the supporting cast. These are some of my go-to glasses, and they will work for just about any type of drink you mix up. You'll find all of these featured on different carts throughout the book:

- beer glass or mug

- copper mug

- cordial glass

- coupe

- double old fashioned or rocks

- flute

- goblet

- highball or collins

- Nick and Nora martini glass

- wineglass

Nº.1
CLASSIC CART

The golden age of classic cocktails overlapped with the Gilded Age, and a cart dedicated to those classic drinks should evoke the era. Rich textures and deep colors, as well as warm wood can re-create an aura of old-fashioned and lavish hospitality. To balance the classic feel with a modern sensibility, look to modern prints, like a patterned wallpaper, and simple furniture without any embellishment.

This was the era when classic cocktails reigned. Stock your vintage cart with bottles of bourbon, rye, vermouth, and bitters, to give yourself lots of options to re-create it.

VERY CHERRY MANHATTAN

2 oz [60 ml] rye whiskey or bourbon

½ oz [15 ml] sweet vermouth

½ oz [15 ml] cherry liqueur or cherry juice

1 dash orange or aromatic bitters

3 Luxardo maraschino cherries for garnish

1. Add the rye, sweet vermouth, cherry liqueur, and bitters to a mixing glass with ice.

2. Stir and strain into a cocktail glass.

3. Garnish with 3 maraschino cherries.

Honey Old Fashioned: 2 oz [60 ml] whiskey, 1½ tsp honey, 2 dashes aromatic bitters, 1 lemon peel and 1 Luxardo maraschino cherry for garnish. Combine the whiskey, honey, and bitters in a mixing glass and add ice. Stir and strain into a rocks glass filled with ice. Garnish with lemon and Luxardo cherry.

Grapefruit Scofflaw: 1½ oz [45 ml] rye, 1 oz [30 ml] dry vermouth, ½ oz [15 ml] fresh lime juice, ½ oz [15 ml] grenadine, ½ oz [15 ml] fresh grapefruit juice, 1 dash orange bitters, 1 grapefruit twist for garnish. Combine the liquid ingredients in a shaker, add ice, and shake. Strain into a coupe glass and garnish with the grapefruit twist.

Glassware like a collins, old fashioned, and coupe are timeless, and having a variety on hand makes it easy to serve classic cocktails with style. Mixed glassware that share a rich design element, such as gold details, ensures a coordinated look, even if you're serving a number of different drinks throughout the evening. You can keep the theme going with your bar tools, so that the whole scene is artfully styled even when not in use.

If you're serving a variety of drinks, you'll want to keep ice at the ready, instead of running back and forth to the freezer. Storing it in a luxe ice bucket gives it the star treatment it deserves. Most buckets come with a set of tongs, but I suggest you invest in a few extra. That way your guests can mix their own drinks without having to wait in line.

No.2
VODKA CART

Y

Vodka is a neutral spirit and if it's the one you prefer to stock, consider a bar that reflects a neutral and minimalist aesthetic. Plus a cool and refined space creates a visual retreat during cocktail hour. Look for furniture with clean lines, such as a glass bar top, clear glassware, and monochromatic decor—white curtains, black and white bar towels, and books—to create a simple and airy feel. Sheer curtains, meanwhile, lend a feminine, warm touch that softens any harder edges.

Complement these neutral hues with one or two pops of color to create a pulled-together look. Flowers or fruit can easily be added whenever the mood strikes.

CITRUS VODKA TONIC

2 orange slices

½ oz [15 ml] simple syrup (page 12)

1½ oz [45 ml] citrus-flavored vodka

1 oz [30 ml] Fever Tree Mediterranean Tonic or other floral tonic water

1. Place the orange slices in a cocktail shaker and muddle with the simple syrup.

2. Add the vodka and ice and shake vigorously.

3. Strain into a cocktail glass, top with tonic, and stir.

Olive Oil Martini: 2½ oz [75 ml] vodka, ½ oz [15 ml] dry vermouth, 6 drops olive oil, 1 olive for garnish. Combine the vodka and vermouth in a mixing glass and add ice. Stir and strain into a martini glass. Drizzle the olive oil on top, and garnish with the olive.

Grapefruit and Lillet Spritzer: 1¾ oz [50 ml] citrus vodka, ½ oz [15 ml] Lillet Blanc, 2 oz [60 ml] fresh grapefruit juice, ½ oz [15 ml] simple syrup (page 12), 1 oz [30 ml] soda water, 1 thyme sprig and 1 grapefruit slice for garnish. Combine the liquid ingredients, except for the soda water, in a shaker. Add ice and shake. Strain into a collins glass filled with ice, and top with soda water. Garnish with the thyme and grapefruit slice.

Measuring your ingredients accurately is crucial and sets a great drink apart from a good one. Buy a metal jigger or a measured shot glass to ensure a perfect cocktail every time.

Your barware can do more than just mix and measure. Shaker tins double as vases to hold fresh flowers, and beautiful swizzle sticks or muddlers can sit on display as decorative touches.

№.3

RUM CART

RUM CART

Rum conjures up images of tropical drinks, so a rum-themed bar can lean into that idea. For your decor, choose bold patterns like palm-print wallpaper and green accents to transport your guests to a tropical oasis while you mix and sip. Luxe metallic details add warmth and pair perfectly with the lavish tropical drinks. Whether it's a gold cart or metallic details on your glassware, incorporating warm metals into whimsical decor will set the stage for exotic rum cocktails.

MINTY MOJITO

1 oz [30 ml] fresh lime juice

2 tsp superfine sugar

10 mint leaves, plus 1 small sprig
(5 to 6 leaves) for garnish

2 oz [60 ml] white rum

1 oz [30 ml] club soda

1. In a collins glass, stir together the lime juice and sugar until the sugar dissolves.

2. Rub a mint leaf over the rim of the glass, and then tear all the leaves in half and toss into the glass.

3. Add the rum, and fill the glass with crushed ice. Top off with the club soda. Gently stir for 5 seconds, and garnish with the mint sprig.

Pineapple Rum Swizzle: 2 oz [60 g] aged rum, 1 oz [30 g] fresh lime juice, 1 oz [30 g] fresh pineapple juice, ½ oz [15 g] orgeat or simple syrup (page 12), 1 mint sprig (5 to 6 leaves) and 3 pineapple leaves for garnish. Combine the liquid ingredients in a cocktail glass and add crushed ice. Stir with a spoon or swizzle stick until frosty. Garnish with the mint sprig and pineapple leaves.

Coconut Cooler: 1 oz [30 ml] dark rum, 1 oz [30 ml] light rum, 2 oz [60 ml] unsweetened coconut cream, 1 oz [30 ml] fresh pineapple juice, ¼ oz [7.5 ml] fresh lime juice, ½ oz [15 ml] orgeat syrup, 1 oz [30 ml] club soda, 1 lime twist and 1 mint sprig (5 to 6 leaves) for garnish. Combine all the liquid ingredients, except for the club soda, in a shaker and add ice. Shake and strain into a tall glass filled with ice. Top with the club soda and garnish with the lime and mint.

If you want to stick to a single color, consider incorporating it into your decor and glassware. Using different shades of the same color—such as the green used here—in barware and cushions helps carry the theme. Add pieces in a contrasting tone, like crisp white, to draw the eye. It's a great way to show off coveted collected items like antique vases and decanters.

If your bar cart is getting too crowded with glasses and bottles, consider adding hanging racks to one of the bar's shelves to store the extra bottles. It adds storage space without requiring an additional shelf. You'll have more room to display vintage barware and beautifully designed bottles and can artfully display each item instead of cramming everything together.

№ 4

TEQUILA CART

A fun way to embrace tequila is with bright, saturated colors to match the colorful spirit of Mexico, tequila's home country. The vibrant red-patterned wallpaper behind this cart, which takes its inspiration from the embroidered textiles of the Otomi people, gives passion and energy to a room. To make a statement against the bright pattern, choose a sturdy cart that won't disappear into the background; the wooden one here recalls the rustic wooden furniture of the Southwest and Mexico. Stock tequila of different ages—blanco, reposado, and añejo—to make a variety of drinks for your fiestas. And keep some vintage seltzer bottles at the ready to make long, refreshing tequila drinks rather than the ones that leave you with regrets the next day.

PALOMA

Juice of ½ red grapefruit

1½ oz [45 ml] reposado tequila

1 Tbsp agave syrup or simple syrup (page 12), optional

½ cup [65 g] flaky sea salt

½ lime

1 oz [30 ml] club soda

1. Combine the grapefruit juice, tequila, and syrup, if using, in a mixing glass and stir until well combined.

2. Cover a small plate with the sea salt. Rub the lime along the rim of a tall glass and press it into the salt until well coated.

3. Pour the grapefruit and tequila mixture into the glass, add ice, and top with club soda. Squeeze any extra lime juice into your drink and enjoy.

Tequila Sunset: 2 oz [60 ml] reposado tequila, 2 oz [60 ml] fresh grapefruit juice, 1 oz [30 ml] orange juice, ¼ oz [7.5 ml] orgeat syrup, ½ oz [15 ml] pomegranate grenadine, and 1 maraschino cherry, 1 orange slice, and 1 grapefruit slice for garnish. Combine the tequila, juices, and syrup in a shaker and add ice. Shake and strain into an ice-filled collins glass. Slowly pour in the grenadine and garnish with the fruit.

Mean Green Cooler: 3 jalapeño slices, 12 cilantro leaves, 2 oz [60 ml] blanco tequila, 1 oz [30 ml] fresh cucumber juice, 2 oz [60 ml] fresh lime juice, 1 Tbsp agave syrup, 1 oz [30 ml] ginger beer, 1 cucumber slice and 1 cilantro sprig for garnish. Muddle the jalapeño and cilantro leaves in a shaker. Add the remaining ingredients, except for the garnishes. Add ice and shake. Strain into a collins glass filled with ice. Garnish with the cucumber slice and cilantro sprig.

Tequila is often thought of as a shooter spirit, but it has so much potential in cocktails. Made from the agave plant, it has an earthy, sweet flavor that pairs beautifully with citrus. Keep some bowls of lemons, limes, oranges, and grapefruit on hand, both to add to drinks and to provide pops of saturated yellow, green, and orange to your space.

Plants add a fresh touch to any bar cart, and they can also help carry a cart's theme, especially here. The agave plant is part of the succulent family, and succulents are just the thing for giving some life and lovely texture to your bar cart. Gather them in a variety of colors and shapes and plant them in a container that can sit on your cart. Succulents are almost impossible to kill; they can withstand heat and require little watering—the perfect plant!

Nº.5

WHISKEY CART

Whiskey is an approachable spirit—no leather-bound books or smoking jacket required. Like many spirits, it has a variety of expressions, each with its own characteristics. From sweet bourbon to smoky and peaty scotch, to spicy rye there is a style for just about every person's tastes. Stock a few different kinds, and you'll have the right one for any guest or occasion—a good strategy for a single-spirit cart.

Despite its name, a bar cart does not need wheels and it may not have been designed to hold drinks. You can turn a sturdy sideboard or family antique table into a bar station to display your favorite whiskeys and striking barware.

WHISKEY WARMER

1½ oz [45 ml] rye whiskey

1 oz [30 ml] applejack or Calvados

¾ oz [22.5 ml] fresh lemon juice

¾ oz [22.5 ml] simple syrup (page 12)

4 dashes Angostura bitters

Splash of club soda

Lemon twist for garnish

1. Combine all the ingredients but the club soda in a cocktail shaker, fill with ice, and shake for about 30 seconds.

2. Pour into an ice-filled rocks glass, top off with club soda, and stir.

3. Garnish with the lemon twist.

Honey Whiskey Sour: 2 oz [60 ml] whiskey, 1¼ oz [37.5 ml] fresh lemon juice, 1 oz [30 ml] honey syrup (page 12), 1 egg white, 1 lemon wheel, and 1 Luxardo or brandied cherry for garnish. Combine the liquid ingredients in a shaker and shake (see page 11 for details of the dry shake method). Add ice and shake again. Strain into an ice-filled rocks glass, and garnish with the lemon and cherry.

Scofflaw: 1½ oz [45 ml] rye, 1 oz [30 ml] vermouth, ¾ oz [22.5 ml] real grenadine syrup, ¾ oz [22.5 ml] fresh lime juice, 1 dash bitters, 1 orange twist for garnish. Combine all the liquid ingredients in a shaker, add ice, and shake. Strain into a coupe and garnish with the orange twist.

If your bar cart lacks storage, it's good to have bar tools that look chic on display. Investing in matching pieces, like the metallic bar tools for this cart, creates a unified look that you'll want to show off. Gold is a classic choice, but rose gold adds a slightly modern, feminine touch to the otherwise neutral space. Sleek glass decanters can display your favorite whiskeys and keep them at the ready, rather than hiding them in a cabinet.

№.6

GIN CART

Gin may be clear, but it is far from neutral. Although it is always distilled with juniper, gin has many different expressions and styles. Its bold, coniferous taste is a natural pairing with herbs and citrus.

To go with a clear spirit like gin, keep things fresh and bright in white, silver, and clear glass. That doesn't mean your bar space has to look boring. With all neutral decor, it's important to have a mix of textures and shapes—round and sharp, soft and hard, metal and glass, along with natural elements like flowers. All-white decor can feel a little cold, but adding a cozy rug, like this pale faux sheepskin, brings texture and warmth to the space.

GIN & JAM

2 oz [60 ml] herbaceous, juniper-forward gin

¾ oz [22.5 ml] fresh lemon juice

½ oz [15 ml] simple syrup (page 12)

1½ tsp of the best apricot jam you can find

1. Combine all the ingredients in a cocktail shaker, add ice, and shake.

2. Double strain (see page 11) into a cocktail glass.

Minty Gin Rickey: 1 mint sprig (5 to 6 leaves) plus 1 mint sprig for garnish, 2 oz [60 ml] gin, ½ oz [15 ml] fresh lime juice, 2 oz [60 ml] soda water, 2 lime wheels for garnish. Run 1 mint sprig around the inside of a collins glass and discard. Combine the remaining ingredients, except the garnishes, in the glass. Fill with ice and stir. Garnish with the lime wheels and remaining mint sprig.

Mixed Words: ¾ oz [22.5 ml] gin, ¾ oz [22.5 ml] Yellow Chartreuse, ¾ oz [22.5 ml] maraschino liqueur, ¾ oz [22.5 ml] fresh lemon juice, 1 lemon twist for garnish. Combine the liquid ingredients in a shaker, add ice, and shake. Strain into a coupe glass and garnish with the lemon twist.

One large statement piece of art above the polished bar cart, in the same color scheme as your decor, lends interest to the clean lines and neutral palette. If it's intriguing or unusual, it also provides a conversation piece for friends and guests at parties.

Nº 7

PUNCH CART

If you're going to serve a single drink to a group of guests, an excellent party choice, translate this idea to your decor as well. Choose one hue and use it in varying shades for an easy way to bring color into a room. On this cart, pink hues are picked up in the glassware, flowers, and displayed bottles, instead of party hats or disposable decor. When the party is over, you can put some items away and display pieces in other colors.

To make it easy to throw a party at the last minute, keep non-alcoholic mixers on hand so you can create impromptu punches. Just add spirits and the juice from whatever fruits you have around, and you are party ready in a flash.

SPRING GARDEN PUNCH

12 oz [350 ml] of your favorite vodka

3 Tbsp St. Germain liqueur or simple syrup (page 12)

1 bottle [750 ml] sparkling rosé

FOR THE ICE MOLD:

1 pt [300 g] fresh strawberries, with stems on, quartered

4 rosemary sprigs, cut into 1-in [2.5-cm] pieces

TO MAKE THE ICE MOLD:

1. Place the cut strawberries in a bowl or cake pan, preferably one with a flat bottom, smaller than the size of your punch bowl. Arrange the rosemary sprigs evenly around the strawberry pieces, and tuck a few under the berries if desired.

2. Add water until the bowl is ¼ full and the strawberries and rosemary are mostly submerged in water.

3. Cover and place in the freezer for at least 2 hours or until frozen solid. You can make this ice mold up to three days in advance and keep it in the freezer.

TO MAKE THE PUNCH:

1. Combine the vodka and St. Germain in a punch bowl and stir to combine.

2. Add the ice mold and top with sparkling rosé. Serve in coupes or rocks glasses.

MAKES 8 DRINKS

Sparkling Honeyed Grapefruit Punch: 10 oz [300 ml] gin, 20 oz [600 ml] grapefruit juice, 5 oz [150 ml] fresh lemon juice, ⅓ cup + 1 tsp [135 g] honey, 20 oz [600 ml] sparkling wine, 10 rosemary sprigs, and 1 sliced grapefruit for garnish. Combine all the ingredients but the garnishes in a punch bowl, add an ice mold or ice, and stir. Float the garnishes on the punch. Serve in rocks glasses. MAKES 10 DRINKS

Rose Rosé Punch: 24 strawberries, 24 raspberries, 10 oz [300 ml] citrus-flavored vodka, 1 bottle [750 ml] rosé, 16 drops rose water, 8 oz [240 ml] fresh lemon juice, 8 oz [240 ml] soda water, and rose petals for garnish. In a large shaker, muddle 18 of the strawberries and 18 of the raspberries with vodka. Shake and strain into a punch bowl, and add an ice mold or ice. Add the remaining liquid ingredients and stir. Float the remaining 6 strawberries and 6 raspberries and the rose petals on top. MAKES 10 DRINKS

You don't have to be a florist to keep lovely bouquets in the house. A vase filled with one type of flower in varying shades makes an effortless but attractive arrangement. Alternatively, you can create the same effect by choosing different flowers in the same shade. Both options create a look that is unified without being monotonous.

In the course of a party, punches can become watered down if you're using plain ice. Instead, create a large ice mold by combining fruits, herbs, and fresh juice in a Bundt cake pan, bread pan, or other large dish and freezing them. When you use the same ingredients and flavors in the ice mold that are in the punch, the ice will enhance the punch even as it melts.

№ 8

BEER CART

If beer is your choice of drink, look for a cart with deep, waterproof sides so the cart can be filled with ice and double as an ice bucket. If the sides are not waterproof, line them with plastic to protect them from the melting ice. Whether you and your guests are drinking lagers, pilsners, and sours on a hot day, or stouts and porters on a chilly day, it's always a good time to crack open a beer!

To decorate the rest of your space, look to beer labels for inspiration. They are often colorful and graphic, with great typography. Look for items that mimic the eye-catching packaging, like bold signs. You can also display a beautiful bike, sports balls, or a surfboard and have decor that doubles as storage.

MICHELADA

2 Tbsp Tajín seasoning or Himalayan pink salt

2 oz [60 ml] tomato juice

1 oz [30 ml] fresh lime juice, plus 1 lime wedge for wetting the mug

1 tsp hot sauce

2 dashes Worcestershire sauce

One 12-oz [360 ml] bottle of your favorite lager

1. Sprinkle 1 Tbsp of the Tajín on a small plate. Rub a wedge of lime around the rim of your beer mug and then press it into the Tajín.

2. Combine the remaining 1 Tbsp of Tajín, the tomato juice, lime juice, hot sauce, and Worcestershire sauce in a beer mug and stir to blend well.

3. Top with the lager.

Sour Shandy: 6 oz [180 ml] ginger beer, 4 oz [120 ml] lemonade, 10 oz [300 ml] sour beer, 1 lemon wheel for garnish. Combine the ginger beer and lemonade in a large beer glass. Pour the sour beer over and stir. Garnish with the lemon wheel.

Pineapple Beer Fizz: 6 oz [180 ml] fresh pineapple juice, 2 oz [60 ml] soda water, 1 squeeze of lime, 8 oz [240 ml] German pilsner or lager, 1 lime wheel for garnish. Combine the pineapple juice, soda water, and squeeze of lime in a large beer glass. Pour the beer over and stir. Garnish with the lime wheel.

Beer, with its refreshing and cooling qualities, is the perfect pairing to anything spicy and salty. Offer bowls of nuts and savory snack mixes that have an added punch of heat, or serve spicy beer cocktails that have a kick!

№.9
WINE CART

Wine is a universally celebrated spirit and it is also a broad category with lots of rich flavors, from champagne, rosé, and pinot, to fortified wines like sherry. Wine makes an excellent anchor for a bar cart that can change with the season, just like your selection of wines.

In warmer weather look to stock light linens that can double as impromptu napkins, and in the cooler months, store piles of blankets on the cart to grab when it gets drafty outside. Fresh flowers are lovely in spring and summer, while freshly cut branches are a simple yet striking addition to a room during fall and winter. Simply swap in the seasonally appropriate items without overhauling your whole cart.

WINTERY MULLED WINE

2 tsp black peppercorns, lightly crushed

1 tsp fennel seeds, lightly crushed

1 small nutmeg

1 bottle [750 ml] fruity red wine, such as zinfandel or merlot

1½ cups [300 g] dark brown sugar

3 bay leaves

Strips of zest from 1 orange

¼ cup [85 g] honey

1. Put the peppercorns, fennel seeds, and nutmeg in a large tea ball or wrap them in cheesecloth and secure them with kitchen string.

2. In a large saucepan, combine the aromatics with the wine, brown sugar, bay leaves, orange zest, and honey. Cover and simmer over low heat for 10 minutes. Remove from the heat and let stand, covered, for 30 minutes.

MAKES 5 DRINKS

Fall Sangria: 1 lemon, 1 pear, 2 figs, 1 bottle [750 ml] pinot or another red wine, 4 oz [120 ml] tawny port, 2 oz [60 ml] pear brandy, 8 oz [240 ml] apple juice, 2 oz [60 ml] simple syrup (page 12), 1 cinnamon stick, 4 oz [120 ml] soda water. Slice the fruit. Combine all the ingredients in a pitcher and let sit in the fridge overnight. Serve in wineglasses over ice.
MAKES 8 DRINKS

Summer Sherry Cobble: 2 orange slices, 5 raspberries, 3 strawberries, 4 oz [120 ml] sherry, 2 oz [60 ml] simple syrup (page 12). Muddle 1 orange slice, 4 raspberries, and 2 strawberries in a shaker. Add the sherry and simple syrup and shake. Strain into cocktail glasses filled with crushed ice. Garnish with 1 raspberry, 1 strawberry, and 1 orange slice.
MAKES 1 DRINK

Goblets are a universal glass for almost any type of wine, and for warm and chilled wine cocktails, too. A set of goblets or a mix-and-match collection doubles as cart decoration, as do antique wine bottles with unique shapes and decanters in varying sizes to create height and visual interest on the cart. Add a geometric wine rack to keep your favorite vintages organized and in sight.

There has never been a more delicious pair than wine and cheese, and a cheese plate is a guaranteed crowd-pleaser. Don't let the idea of creating one stress you out. Set out a few different styles of cheese with charcuterie, fruit, and crackers or bread to graze on while you and your guests sip your favorite wine. A snack plate is also a great way to utilize the top of your cart if you don't want to fill it with different bottles.

№ 10

LOW-PROOF CART

Low-proof cocktails are perfect for brunch, picnics, long parties, and for when you want a tipple with less buzz. Lower-proof spirits like Pimm's and Aperol add lots of bright flavor without packing the alcoholic punch.

Bold is the name of the decorating game here; low alcohol content doesn't mean less fun. A brightly colored cart can make a big statement and work harmoniously with other colors. The key is to pick one dominant hue, like the yellow used here, and add accent colors in similarly bright tones. For small places consider a three-tiered design instead of the usual two tiers, to provide extra storage space.

PIMM'S CUP

2 oz [60 ml] Pimm's No. 1

3 oz [90 ml] ginger ale or lemonade

1 cucumber wheel and 1 lemon wheel

1 mint sprig (5 to 6 leaves)

1. Pour the Pimm's into an ice-filled collins glass and top with the ginger ale.

2. Garnish with the cucumber wheel, lemon wheel, and mint sprig and serve.

Cucumber Spritz: One 2-in [5-cm] piece of cucumber (sliced) plus 1 cucumber wheel for garnish, ¼ oz [7.5 ml] Aperol, 3 oz [90 ml] champagne, 1 oz [30 ml] soda water. Muddle the sliced cucumber in a shaker with the Aperol. Double strain (see page 11) into a wineglass filled with ice. Top with champagne and soda water and stir. Garnish with cucumber.

Pimm's Sparkler: 1 oz [30 ml] Pimm's No. 1, 2 oz [60 ml] fresh orange juice, 3 oz [90 ml] champagne, 1 long orange peel for garnish. Combine the Pimm's and orange juice in a flute. Top with champagne and stir. Garnish with the orange peel.

Bring some fun to your cart with extra decorations and unique touches. Abstract
cocktail napkins give an artistic touch and offer a low-cost alternative to investing
in works of art for your walls. Dominos and games stowed in colorful or vintage
boxes make for lively decor, and the games can be broken out and enjoyed during
the party.

Make your own fizzy water at home by using a soda siphon with a contemporary look, stashed on or near the cart. Choose some interesting juices or make your own to add to the mix, and use fresh garnishes to accent your drinks. Then serve in your most colorful glassware; this is its time to shine!

Nº. II

KIDS CART

KIDS CART

Why let the adults have all of the fun, when you can arrange a kid-friendly cart for birthdays and every day! If you're looking for something that stands up to messes and spills, choose a metal cart and paint it in a vivid color if it needs to be jazzed up—it will be easier to clean those sticky hand prints off the sides. Just because it's alcohol-free doesn't mean you can't have options. A fruity sipper and a creamy, dessertlike drink are sure to be pleasers.

SODA DROP

8 oz [240 ml] fresh juice, such as orange, guava, or mango

3 oz [90 ml] sparkling water

1 fruit stick or Twizzler for garnish

1. Pour the juice into a tall glass and top with sparkling water.

2. Garnish with a fruit stick.

Kiwi-Pineapple Lemonade: ½ kiwi with skin removed plus 1 slice for garnish, 3 oz [90 ml] fresh pineapple juice, 2 oz [60 ml] lemonade. Muddle the kiwi in a collins glass or tall cup and add ice. Add the pineapple juice and lemonade and stir. Garnish with the kiwi slice.

Salted Caramel Chocolate Milkshake: 1½ cups [300 g] chocolate ice cream, 2 oz [60 ml] milk, 1 Tbsp caramel sauce, sea salt. Blend the ice cream and milk in a blender. Pour into a collins glass and drizzle with the caramel sauce. Sprinkle sea salt on top.

When there's a party, especially one for kids, there is probably going to be cake (maybe an adorable donut stack like the one shown here). So for drinks, sparkling and natural-flavored sodas that are lower in sugar might be a good option to balance the sweet cake and candy. Colorful juices that are naturally vibrant—like orange, mango, guava, watermelon, and pomegranate—also make the drinks bright and cheerful. Add a fun touch to kids' drinks, or any drinks, with striped paper straws, which look great stored on the cart in a colorful cup.

A cart is more than just a place to store fixings for drinks. It's a place to display your cake and candy favors, and to collect party items like hats and noisemakers. Use the shelves to store games and activities for kids of all ages in one area, so they're easy to find. Choose classic party staples in modern graphic patterns if you can get away with it, so that you can use any leftovers at an event for adults.

N°. 12

CRATE CART

No cart? No problem! If you have some wooden crates, you can stack them together to make an impromptu bar cart. They're simple to collect at flea markets, make a fun statement, and produce an easy-to-reorganize modular design. Divided boxes corral your must-have bottles like whiskey, rum, tequila, and Jägermeister, as well as bar tools and cocktail recipe books. Crates turned on their sides can display artwork, collections, or eye-catching bar accessories.

Whip up drinks that are easy to throw together so you can spend more time catching up and watching the game. Serve up frosty beer and cold cocktails in stylish mugs, which keep drinks chilled and your hands warm. And use the space behind the bar for displaying artwork—it's the perfect backdrop.

MOSCOW MULE

2 oz [60 ml] vodka

1 Tbsp fresh lime juice

4 oz [120 ml] chilled ginger beer

1 lime wedge

1. Combine the vodka and lime juice in an ice-filled copper mule mug. Pour over the ginger beer and stir to mix.

2. Garnish with the lime wedge.

Peanut Rum and Coke: 1 cup [140 g] peanuts, 16 oz [480 ml] aged rum, 5 oz [150 ml] cola. To make peanut-infused rum, combine the peanuts and rum in a jar and set aside, covered, for 4 days. Strain through a tea strainer into a clean jar. Makes 16 oz [480 ml] of peanut-infused rum. For 1 drink, pour 2 oz [60 ml] of the peanut rum into an ice-filled cocktail rocks or collins glass. Top with the cola and stir. Store the extra infused rum in a sealed container for up to 3 months.

Bittersweet Float: 1 oz [30 ml] Fernet-Branca or Jägermeister, 1 oz [30 ml] bourbon, 6 oz [180 ml] root beer, 1 cup [200 g] vanilla ice cream. Combine the spirits in a large glass. Top with the root beer and then the ice cream. Slip in a straw and enjoy.

QUEENS
FOREST HILLS
COURT ST
BORO HALL

BROOKLYN

Decorating doesn't have to be fancy or expensive. You can combine eye-catching items you already own with your cocktail bottles and bar tools to make a statement. Display flasks and valuables like watches and cufflinks in decorative boxes. They provide a built-in frame, and keep things from looking cluttered. Sculptural liquor bottles, like skulls, do double duty as a cocktail ingredient and part of your decor. Other mementos from your favorite hobbies—an old skateboard, boxing gloves, or a camera—add personality to the space.

№ 13

HOLIDAY CART

HOLIDAY CART

The holidays are chock-full of entertaining, celebrating, and of course, enjoying cocktails. Let your bar cart take center stage at your annual holiday fête and look for a unique modern shape—it can make a big impact. The round cart shown here echoes the shape of an ornament, making it doubly cute for the holiday season.

If you love a theme, the holidays are a great time to really lean into the glitz and glamour. Gold or silver provides a festive, shimmering accent color, and when paired with pops of rich red, it makes an otherwise neutral space look festive. You can keep the place feeling warm with fabrics, in this case a faux fur rug and a large, cozy chair for settling in on a cold winter's evening with a nightcap.

THE CANDY CANE

1½ oz [45 ml] gin

¾ oz [22.5 ml] Chambord or cherry liqueur

Splash of sparkling wine

1 small candy cane or maraschino cherry for garnish

1. Combine the gin and Chambord in a shaker, add ice, and shake until combined.

2. Strain into a cocktail glass and top with the sparkling wine.

3. Garnish with a candy cane or cherry.

Cranberry-Orange Sparkler: 1½ oz [45 ml] gin, 3 oz [90 ml] fresh orange juice, 1 oz [30 ml] cranberry juice, ¼ oz [7.5 ml] Leopold Bros. Aperitivo or other bitter aperitif, ¼ oz [7.5 ml] Cointreau, ½ oz [15 ml] simple syrup (page 12), 1 orange twist for garnish. Combine all the liquid ingredients in a shaker and add ice. Shake and strain into an ice-filled cocktail glass with ice. Garnish with the orange twist.

Pear 75: 1 oz (30 g) gin, ½ oz (15 ml) pear liqueur, ½ oz (15 ml) fresh lemon juice, 4 oz (120 ml) champagne, and 1 lemon twist, 1 cranberry, and 1 rosemary sprig for garnish. Combine the liquid ingredients in a shaker, add ice, and shake. Strain into a champagne flute. Garnish with the lemon twist, cranberry, and rosemary.

Keep a variety of glassware styles on your cart to serve different types of beverages at your holiday parties. A mix of champagne flutes, coupes, double old fashioneds, wineglasses, and other stemware will accommodate the classic holiday cocktails. If you like to throw large parties—or some of your friends are a little clumsy—consider thick, goblet-like champagne flutes instead of delicate stemware.

Display color-coordinated liquor bottles in a festive color on the top shelf to bring out the holiday theme. Sparkling wine should have a permanent home on the bar cart during the holidays; celebratory champagne cocktails and glasses of bubbly are a must!

Candles are a classic way to set the mood at a soirée, but they can be messy or precarious depending on your space and guests. For a modern no-fuss approach, string towering birch branches with twinkling lights to lend a glimmering ambiance to a room.

Nᵒ. 14

CREDENZA CART

If a typical bar cart doesn't give you enough storage space, remember that most furniture with a flat surface can serve as a bar cart, too. Vintage wooden credenzas and sideboards have character and are the perfect pieces for stocking your home bar. Choose something with a long top for displaying your favorite bottles, florals, and a bowl of fresh fruit for garnishes. Down below, cabinets house mixers and other liqueurs, and the cabinet doors can be closed to hide clutter and keep things streamlined. Drawers are also a plus for tucking away bar necessities such as cocktail napkins, picks, bar tools, platters, and place settings for entertaining. You can easily swap in items to match your current theme or party and stash the things you don't want to display.

KUMQUAT & GIN

3 kumquats or other small citrus fruit, sliced

2 oz [60 ml] gin

4 oz [120 ml] tonic water

1. Put one sliced kumquat in a tall glass.

2. Muddle slightly. Fill the glass with ice and place the rest of the kumquat slices on top.

3. Add the gin and tonic, stir, and enjoy.

Spiced Nut: 2 oz [60 ml] Nocino or other walnut liqueur, 1½ tsp brown sugar, 1½ oz [45 ml] rum, 2 dashes cinnamon or aromatic bitters, 1 orange twist for garnish. Combine everything but the orange twist in a shaker and add ice. Shake and strain into a coupe glass. Garnish with the orange twist.

Creamsicle Fizz: 2 oz [60 ml] gin, 1 oz [30 ml] fresh orange juice, ½ oz [15 ml] simple syrup (page 12), 1 egg white, 1 oz [30 ml] heavy cream, 1 oz [30 ml] soda water, 1 orange wheel for garnish. Combine the gin, juice, syrup, and egg white in a shaker and dry shake for 3 minutes. Add ice and cream to the shaker and shake for 1 minute, or until the ice dissolves. Strain into a collins glass and top with soda water. Garnish with the orange wheel.

Trays are helpful to group bottles and serving bowls and define space on a large surface. Items gathered together on a tray look intentional and put together, rather than haphazard. If your problem is not enough space, select glassware and bar tools that stack to save room. Make use of what you have—when not holding a drink, stemmed glasses can double as decorative vases for small arrangements and blooms. And use the back of the surface to display artwork—you can easily swap it in and out to show off new favorites.

№.15

ITALIAN CART

If you're building your cart theme around a country or geographic region, consider what kind of drinks are popular in that area. This cart takes inspiration from Italy, and the bottles and glassware make it easy to mix up drinks that are popular there.

Don't stop at just the drinks; incorporate the theme into your decor as well. Here there are heirlooms and antique furniture that evoke a European feel, and an Italian metal fan that doubles as a statement piece and a way to keep cool on a blistering hot day. Bursts of orange are inviting and pay homage to the abundant citrus along the Italian coastline. Use the cart to build a sense of place and create cocktails that take you there with the first sip.

AMERICANO

2 oz [60 ml] sweet vermouth

2 oz [60 ml] Campari

1 oz [30 ml] club soda

1 orange wedge for garnish

1. Combine the vermouth and Campari in an ice-filled cocktail glass and stir.

2. Top with club soda, stir, and garnish with the orange wedge.

Cocchi Grapefruit Spritz: 3 oz [90 ml] prosecco, 2 oz [60 ml] Cocchi Americano, 2 oz [60 ml] grapefruit juice, 1 oz [30 ml] soda water, 1 grapefruit slice for garnish. Combine the liquid ingredients in an ice-filled stemmed glass and stir. Garnish with the grapefruit slice.

Cynar Flip: 2½ ounces [75 ml] Cynar 70 or Cynar, 1 egg, ½ oz [15 ml] simple syrup (page 12), 1 pinch cinnamon. Combine the Cynar, egg, and syrup in a shaker and add ice. Shake and strain into a coupe glass. Dust with cinnamon.

If you generally like to make batches of drinks, look for a large mixing glass, like the mid-century, lab-inspired one on the facing page, which can double as a pitcher to serve refreshing aperitif cocktails.

Clear glass goblets can really show off drinks, including the Italian favorite, an Aperol spritz, but they're best used for lower-proof drinks and ice-heavy cocktails. Otherwise keep your pours small; a larger glass can make it hard to gauge a serving size.

No. 16

TRAY CART

If you have been peering at all the other carts and are thinking that you just don't have room for one, this is for you! A small space does not have to mean sacrificing a bar. A tray or tray table can be the perfect cocktail station, and it's easy to set up and take down as needed. With that minimal space, keep only key elements, like spirits, glassware, and an ice bucket to display on the tray. Stock just a few bottles, and rely on juices and fresh ingredients from the fridge to create a variety of drinks.

ELDERFLOWER COOL

5 oz [150 ml] high-quality champagne

¾ oz [22.5 ml] St. Germain liqueur

1. Pour the champagne into a flute and top with the St. Germain.

Sorbet Sparkler: 1 oz [30 ml] gin, 3 oz [90 ml] champagne, ½ cup [75 g] lemon sorbet (or other fruit), and 1 lemon slice, 1 mint sprig (5 to 6 leaves), and 1 strawberry for garnish. Combine the gin and champagne in a coupe glass and stir. Add the sorbet and garnish with the lemon, mint, and strawberry.

Floral Gimlet: 2 oz [60 ml] gin, ½ oz [15 ml] St. Germain, ¼ oz [7.5 ml] simple syrup (page 12), ¾ oz [22.5 ml] fresh lime juice, 1 edible flower (like a nasturtium) for garnish. Combine the liquid ingredients in a shaker, add ice, and shake. Strain into a rocks glass with ice. Garnish with the edible flower.

Embracing your small space doesn't have to mean white walls. A bold patterned wallpaper on an accent wall can make a space seem larger. It also makes a backdrop for your bar tray, or for whatever is placed in front of it. The colorful wall makes neutral items stand out, rather than fading into the background. If you go for a darker background, make sure the pattern is lighter in color to keep the space bright.

№ 17

MODERN CART

With so many bar carts on the market, there are lots of options for a nontraditional shape that makes a statement. This one appears to be a geometric sculpture, but a hidden mirrored compartment unfolds to reveal space for bottles and bar tools. Consider a neutral color like black if you go for a modern and edgy design–it keeps the look more sophisticated. Choose a geometric bar cart for a modern look, or go for a rounded, abstract shape with clean lines. Soft rugs and wood bring a warm and natural feel to a modern space.

FLAMING GINGER

1½ oz [45 ml] whiskey

2 pieces crystallized ginger

2 oz [60 ml] ginger ale (optional)

1. Put a large ice cube in a rocks glass and pour the whiskey over.

2. Skewer the ginger on a cocktail pick and place over the rim of the glass.

3. Top with ginger ale, if you like.

Viscous Hibiscus: 2½ oz [75 ml] bourbon, ⅓ oz [10 ml] hibiscus syrup, dash flower bitters (like Workhorse Rye's flower and cacao), 1 hibiscus flower in syrup for garnish. Combine the bourbon, hibiscus syrup, and bitters in a shaker, add ice, and shake. Strain into a rocks glass with a large ice cube and garnish with the hibiscus flower.

White Old Fashioned: 2 oz [60 ml] white whiskey (unaged), 2 dashes grapefruit bitters, 1 tsp simple syrup (page 12), 1 grapefruit twist for garnish. Stir together the liquid ingredients in a mixing glass filled with ice. Strain into a rocks glass with a large ice cube, and garnish with the grapefruit twist.

New spirits, like craft whiskeys and bitters, are popping up all the time, giving home bartenders more options for unique cocktails. A great way to taste these modern spirits is by starting off with variations on an old fashioned, which highlights spirits and bitters perfectly. Alternatively, pick one of your favorite cocktails and swap in a spirit from a new-to-you distiller to see how it tastes in a cocktail. From there, you can keep adding or omitting ingredients to create a cocktail all your own!

№.18

SIDE CART

SIDE CART

For the occasional imbiber and single sipper, or the ardent minimalist, a petite side table with storage makes for a great minibar. Choose one that matches the color of the wall behind it, and it will blend in and give the area an open feeling. For an art piece, a mobile draws the eye up, adds visual interest, and makes the space appear taller, while keeping your side cart and other surfaces free of clutter. A chair next to the bar cart and a cozy blanket are just the right encouragement to take a load off and enjoy an elixir at the end of the day. Simple and elegant.

WHISKEY & RHUBARB

1 demerara sugar cube

¼ tsp rhubarb bitters

2 oz [60 ml] single malt whiskey

1 orange twist for garnish

1. In a rocks glass, soak the sugar cube in the bitters and muddle to dissolve the sugar. Add the whiskey and stir a couple of times with a spoon to combine.

2. Add a single large cube of ice. Twist the orange peel over the glass to release the oils, wipe the rim, and add the twist to your cocktail. Stir and enjoy.

Sidecar: 2 Tbsp sugar, 1¾ oz [50 ml] Cognac, ¼ oz [7.5 ml] Cointreau, ¼ oz [7.5 ml] fresh lemon juice. Put the sugar on a small plate, wet the rim of a coupe glass, and dip into the sugar. Combine the remaining ingredients in a mixing glass, add ice, and stir. Strain into the coupe.

Peach and Sage: 1¾ oz [50 ml] whiskey, ½ oz [15 ml] fresh lemon juice, 1 oz [30 ml] fresh grapefruit juice, 2 dashes peach bitters, 1 sage leaf for garnish. Combine the liquid ingredients in a shaker, add ice, and shake. Strain into a coupe and garnish with the sage leaf.

For small carts, stocking a few different bitters is an easy way to create a lot of variation in your drinks. They add spices, herbs, and other flavorful notes to a drink without adding much volume, and they can help merge together ingredients with different flavor profiles. Unlike liquor, bitters take up minimal space on a cart. All you need is a cubby to keep your collection organized.

AFTER-EIGHT CART

Any low piece of furniture can become an impromptu cart. Coffee tables have long been used as a space for after-dinner drinks, with everyone gathering around to enjoy sweets and dessert drinks. Put out a variety of fruity and spicy after-dinner liqueurs and serve them as is or combine them with other spirits for a sweet dessert cocktail. Don't feel like you can't embrace pink when it comes to your nighttime decor. When paired with midnight hues or black, pink loses its feminine feel and becomes more moody and dramatic.

CITRUS RUSSIAN

1 oz [30 ml] NOLA coffee liqueur or other less sweet coffee liqueur

1 oz [30 ml] citrus-flavored vodka

1 oz [30 ml] heavy cream

1 orange twist for garnish

1. Combine the coffee liqueur, vodka, and heavy cream in an ice-filled rocks glass and stir.

2. Garnish with the orange twist.

Brandied Pear: 1½ oz [45 ml] Cognac or brandy, ¾ oz [22.5 ml] spiced pear liqueur, ½ oz [15 ml] orgeat syrup, 1 lemon twist for garnish. Combine the liquid ingredients in a shaker and add ice. Shake and strain into a flute. Garnish with the lemon twist.

Spiced Pear, Raspberry, and Coffee Sips: 1½ oz [45 ml] pear liqueur, 1½ oz [45 ml] raspberry liqueur, 1½ oz [45 ml] coffee liqueur, ½ cup [70 g] pistachios per serving. Pour each liqueur into a different vintage shot glass. Add the pistachios to a bowl and enjoy while sipping. MAKES 3 DRINKS

Antique cordial and shot glasses are perfect for a tasting of flavorful liqueurs or for sips of petite cocktails, and they look charming in a mismatched set. Mini-trays or rectangular plates help friends keep track of their after-dinner tipples while everyone is chatting and double as a plate for snacks. Add a small glass vase with brightly colored flowers and alongside the beautiful bottles, trays, and snacks, your after-dinner cart is fully decorated.

Nº.20

WHIMSICAL CART

WHIMSICAL CART

Life can be too serious; it needs a touch of whimsy! Don't be afraid of displaying bright, unique items alongside your cocktail tools. Your personal and even quirky taste can be expressed in one small detail, or it can extend well beyond the bar cart into the space surrounding it. Pops of color in varying tones can be used throughout the scene in a chic way; just be sure to use a color at least twice to give your decor visual cohesion. A delicate cart and a sturdy sideboard, along with neutral-colored books, ground the whimsical pieces here, keeping them from appearing too juvenile and tacky.

SMOKING PINEAPPLE

ROASTED JALAPEÑO PURÉE:

4 jalapeño chiles, stemmed, halved lengthwise, and seeded

2½ Tbsp agave syrup

1 tsp roasted jalapeño purée

2 oz [60 ml] vodka

3 oz [90 ml] fresh pineapple juice

½ oz [15 ml] simple syrup (page 12)

¼ oz [7.5 ml] fresh lime juice

1 jalapeño slice for garnish

1 pineapple leaf for garnish

1. TO MAKE THE ROASTED JALAPEÑO PURÉE: Preheat the broiler. Arrange the jalapeño halves on a baking tray and roast until they begin to blister, about 10 minutes. Remove and let cool.

2. Add the jalapeños to a blender or food processor with the agave syrup and purée. Use immediately or store in a sealed jar in the fridge for up to 1 week.

3. TO MAKE THE COCKTAIL: Combine the roasted jalapeño puree, vodka, pineapple juice, simple syrup, and lime juice in a shaker. Add ice and shake. Double strain (see page 11) into a martini glass or coupe. Garnish with the slice of jalapeño and pineapple leaf.

Piña Melon: ½ cup [40 g] sweetened shredded coconut (toasted), 2 oz [60 ml] vodka, 2 oz [60 ml] fresh pineapple juice, 1 oz [30 ml] fresh watermelon juice, 2 oz [60 ml] coconut milk, ½ oz [15 ml] fresh lime juice, ½ oz [15 ml] simple syrup (page 12), 1 pineapple slice and 1 watermelon slice for garnish. Put the toasted coconut on a small plate. Wet the rim of a goblet and dip in the coconut to create a coconut rim on the glass. Fill with ice. Combine the liquid ingredients in a shaker, add ice, and shake. Strain into the glass and garnish with the pineapple and watermelon slices.

Spicy Pomelo: 3 thin slices jalapeño plus 1 slice for garnish, 2 oz [60 ml] gin, 3 oz [90 ml] fresh grapefruit juice, ½ oz [15 ml] honey syrup (page 12), 1 grapefruit slice for garnish. Muddle 3 jalapeño slices in a shaker with the liquid ingredients. Add ice and shake. Double strain (see page 11) into a collins glass with an ice cube. Garnish with the grapefruit slice and remaining jalapeño slice.

Details are important. Hand-painted bar accessories, like a marbled dish to display vintage tools, add a unique touch. To take the personalization of your bar to a whole new level, add painted details to the cart itself. If you have a color scheme for the cart, an abstract pattern, like watercolor, is a good way to add more color without clashing.

There is a fine line between tchotchkes and a curated collection. By grouping together complementary bar pieces, or other items, they appear purposeful and not haphazard. Select things that carry a similar theme, but don't worry about getting too matchy-matchy. Arranging vibrant glassware in the same shade, like these cerulean coupes and martini glasses, or displaying bar props with similar patterns provide a no-fuss, interesting look. Here the brass pineapple jar, cut crystal cobbler shaker, and tea towel play off of one another's geometric shapes and textures harmoniously.

RESOURCES

BAR CARTS PROVIDED BY/COURTESY OF:

Jonathan Adler, jonathanadler.com

The New Traditionalists, thenewtraditionalists.com

RH, restorationhardware.com

Society Social, societysocial.com

BAR PROPS PROVIDED BY/COURTESY OF:

Cocktail Kingdom, cocktailkingdom.com

Mitchell Gold and Bob Williams, mgbw.com

LIQUOR PROVIDED BY/COURTESY OF:

anCnoc, ancnoc.com

Aperol, aperol.com

Boodles Gin, boodlesgin.com

Bombay Sapphire, bombaysapphire.com

Brancott Estate wines, brancottestate.com

Campari, campari.com

Campo Viejo wines, campoviejo.com

Champagne Taittinger, taittinger.com

Cutty Sark, cutty-sark.com

Dewar's, livetrue.dewars.com

Disaronno, disaronno.com

Domenico Valentino Selections, domenicovalentino.com

Elit by Stoli, elitbystoli.com

Hangar 1 Vodka, hangarone.com

Jacob's Creek wines, jacobscreek.com

Jägermeister, jager.com

Jose Cuervo, cuervo.com

Leopold Bros, leopoldbros.com

Sandeman Port, sandeman.com

St. George Spirits, stgeorgespirits.com

Stranahan's Whiskey, stranahans.com

1800 Tequila, 1800tequila.com

Tincup Whiskey, tincupwhiskey.com

WALLPAPER PROVIDED BY:

Hygge & West, hyggeandwest.com

SPECIAL THANKS TO:

Carlo Geraci, carlosays.com

Eddie Ross, eddieross.com

Holger Keifel, holgerkeifel.com